Philosophical Thinking is Yoga for the Mind®

Also by Wilhelm Schmid

High on Low: Harnessing the Power of Unhappiness

❧

Upper West Side Philosophers, Inc. provides a publication venue for original philosophical thinking steeped in lived life, in line with our motto: *philosophical living & lived philosophy.*

WHAT WE GAIN AS WE GROW OLDER

On Gelassenheit

Translated from the German
by Michael Eskin

WILHELM SCHMID

Upper West Side Philosophers, Inc. ❧ New York

Published by Upper West Side Philosophers, Inc.
P. O. Box 250645, New York, NY 10025, USA
www.westside-philosophers.com / www.yogaforthemind.us

English translation copyright © 2015 by Upper West Side
Philosophers, Inc. First edition published in 2016.
Originally published as: *Gelassenheit: was wir gewinnen, wenn wir
älter werden*, Copyright © Insel Verlag Berlin 2014

Cover Image: Peter Paul Rubens, "Old Woman and Boy With
Candles," c. 1616–1617, used by permission of The Royal Pic-
ture Gallery Mauritshuis, The Hague, Netherlands
The colophon is a registered trademark of
Upper West Side Philosophers, Inc.

Library of Congress Cataloging-in-Publication Data

Schmid, Wilhelm, 1953-
  [Gelassenheit. English]
  What we gain as we grow older : on Gelassenheit / translated
from the German by Michael Eskin.
    pages cm
  ISBN 978-1-935830-31-3 (alk. paper)
  1. Aging--Psychological aspects. 2. Calmness. I. Title.
  BF724.55.A35S36 2016
  155.67--dc23

                        2015010038

Typesetting & design: UWSP, Inc.

CONTENTS

TRANSLATOR'S NOTE ON 'GELASSENHEIT'

(pronounced: 'gue·láh·sen·hite')

The common German noun 'gelassenheit' carries an array of interrelated meanings that it would be virtually impossible to render with any one of its possible English equivalents – such as 'tranquility', 'equanimity', 'serenity', 'mellowness', 'laidbackness', 'placidity', 'relaxedness', 'coolness', 'calmness', 'impassibility' or 'unperturbedness' – without forfeiting its semantic and stylistic richness and breadth, and occluding its panoply of shades and nuances in favor of one or the other, depending on context. Just think of the differences in meaning, style, connotation and cultural purview between 'laidback' and 'serene', 'relaxed' and 'equanimous', 'cool' and 'unperturbed', 'mellow' and 'placid', 'calm' and 'impassible'. Yet all of these mean- ings (and more) are contained and always in play in the single word 'gelassenheit', whose semantic and stylistic gestalt by far exceeds the sum of its parts. That is why, following the example of other foreign terms that have entered the English language in the original (e.g. 'schadenfreude', 'zeitgeist', 'uber', 'sitz- fleisch', 'frisson', 'chutzpah' or 'chi'), I have decided to retain 'gelassenheit' (and its cognate adjective 'gelassen') in the original, in the hope that introducing this term into the English idiom will not only do justice to the word and its meanings, but also broaden and enrich our understanding of and perspective on the real-life phenomena it signifies.[*]

[*] In English translations of the works of twentieth-century German existentialist philosopher Martin Heidegger, 'gelassenheit' is often rendered as 're-leasement' — an inelegant neologism that, in my view, captures neither the mundane, everyday character of 'gelassenheit' (which Heidegger intentionally valorizes), nor the specific human trait(s) that 'gelassenheit' and its adjectival cognate 'gelassen' denote and connote. Just imagine saying: "John approached this problem with *releasement*," or "You gotta be *released*, bro!" or "You ought to take it with a little more *releasement* — look at Buddha, and how *released* he was!" Yet in all of these instances you would use 'gelassenheit' or 'gelassen' in German.

ON GELASSENHEIT

PREFACE

At first, it was merely a phenomenon that baffled me, an observation I couldn't help coming back to. Then, as my fiftieth birthday was approaching, I was invited to give my first public lecture on the issue that wouldn't leave me alone: aging. After I had finished, several elderly members of the audience came up to me and said: "Nice lecture, young man, but you cannot yet possibly know about these things!" Indeed, my reflections were not rooted in my own experience of growing older so much as my mother's. I admired her for the gelassenheit with which she embraced it – so remarkably different from so many others – and I looked over her shoulder in order to learn as much as I could from her in the event that some day it might come in handy. Where did her gelassenheit stem from? How could I, too, attain it one day, in the distant future?

In that lecture I made fun of the very notion of 'growing older': isn't 'older' the comparative form of 'old'? Does this mean that we would rather be 'older' than 'old'? When I am sixty, I boasted, I will certainly not refer to myself as 'older'; being 'old' will be enough for me. And, anyway, I went on – as though I were among the very last to have the privilege of experiencing it – the question of how to deal with aging would soon be but a distant memory of 'old age' at the very point of its disappearance, on which researchers around the globe were busy working. I, for one, was happy to take it in stride and devote all my energy to living with it as gelassen as I possibly could — accepting it without resistance, neither sugarcoating nor vilifying it but, rather, embracing the entire gamut of its comforts and discomforts, its attractive and not-so-attractive aspects, viewing it neither through rose-colored nor tinted glasses but, preferably, through a clear pair. After all, isn't a sober view of things the true privilege of aging?

In the meantime, I, too, have made it: I am sixty now — and that means old. The truth is: it is not easy for me. Gelassen I am not. On my sixtieth birthday, I was overcome by a profound sadness about having to bid farewell to my fifties, a wonderful decade that I wouldn't ever be able to experience again. Ten years earlier, I had already been downcast about saying good-bye to my forties (which had been really intense), especially since I did not expect much from the years to come. Sure, these are only numbers; but they do signify realities that gradually creep up on you, until you are suddenly hit by the realization that the past stretches out, the future contracts and death closes in. No amount of mental preparation can anticipate what it actually feels like when things start getting serious. Catchy one-liners aiming to downplay the severity of aging only go so far: "You are as old as you feel"? Really? Come on, let's face it, usually you're older. And how you feel will change nothing about it – on the contrary, it will only lead you to deceive yourself. True, not all deception is bad, but in this case you will end up doubly disappointed when you realize that all the hip talk notwithstanding the truth will have its way.

For a long time I imagined old age as life spent placidly on a sunny patio, reclining in a deck chair, looking out onto the landscape, at peace with myself and the world. What I am still missing, though, is the patio – and consequently all the rest. Only one thing is certain: I never want to be one of those old geezers who will do anything to stay young, to the point of ridicule. I don't want to become the irate old guy who releases his anger and frustration about his dwindling life upon anything that flourishes. I don't want to set out clad in the armor of self-righteousness, wasting whatever strength I may have left on geriatric attacks on the young, who presumably get everything wrong. In fact, the young, I am convinced, are always right; and even when they are not, they are still right, which is to say: they have all the right in the world to gather their own experiences – good or bad, they will learn from them.

We can only be gelassen about what we accept as true; otherwise, we risk squandering our resources in the futile attempt at denying the reality of what is allegedly untrue, which will remain completely unaffected by it. One aspect of the truth of aging is that more than any other form of becoming it is confronted with transience. It has always been that way, but in the modern world it has become a real nuisance: for if technology can make virtually anything happen, why not eternal youth as well? I, too, would like to have it, but what kind of life would that be? I, too, would like it if life were all rainbows and butterflies, but wouldn't this actually exacerbate the negative and disagreeable? So, rather than wasting my grapeshot on fighting aging, I prefer wearing the life etched into my every crease and wrinkle with confidence.

Learning to live with one's own aging is the new task: making an art of what once was a given — growing older; turning our society's *anti-aging bias* into a true *art of aging* that will enable us to live *with* rather than *against* the inevitable. Such an *art of living with aging* can help us to meet the particular challenges of this life stage in a way that will ensure that even as we get on in years we continue appreciating the beauty and the very gift of life.

The *art of living* has long been my main philosophical topic, not because I have mastered it, but because I need it. The concept of the art of living goes back to antiquity — *techne tou biou* or *techne peri bion* in Greek, *ars vitae* or *ars vivendi* in Latin — and it implies a life consciously and purposefully lived. Often, 'art of living' is taken to mean a kind of footloose and fancy-free existence. Certainly, that is an option for anyone who wishes to pursue it; but it is not an endeavor that deserves to be called an 'art'. A quite different, more sophisticated approach consists in consciously steering and, if need be, creatively redirecting one's life. This kind of awareness is not always possible, nor is it always necessary. For it is enough to stop and reflect from time to time – as, for instance, right now – on the fact that we are all headed for old age. But what does that mean? How does it happen? Where am I at this particular juncture in my life? What am I to expect? How can I prepare myself for it? What lies within my power, and what does not? This is where the art of living comes in, understood as a certain awareness that will allow us to find meaning in this life stage as well, to live consciously and meaningfully, lest the temptation to aimlessly drift along get the better of us.

The problem with aging in the modern world is that it has, for the most part, been viewed as meaningless, as a 'disease' even, which must be detected early and treated aggressively before it can be surgically removed. This negative view of aging as devoid of meaning and requiring massive intervention could be one of the side effects of the modern *Me-ism* epidemic, which preaches the ever-youthful *Me*: *Me*, forever and ever – a longing that is most pointedly articulated in the much-covered 1984 pop anthem-*cum*-battle cry *Forever Young* by Alphaville. However, as soon as one view begins to dominate, competing views are called for, for interpretive monopolies threaten life itself by putting it to sleep. Contradiction alone can revive it. A different approach, then – one that could become the hallmark of a modified, alternative modernity – conceives of aging as rife with meaning. But what exactly is it?

A *natural* sense of aging might consist in the fact that our initiation into the inexorable truth that life is forever on the wane occurs gradually, as though nature itself were intent on being extra careful with its creature, that hypersensitive tyrant called 'human being'. Nature, too, is familiar with the *forever-young-principle*, of course – only in nature this principle operates in a completely different way from modern culture, for it is nature itself that remains forever young in letting old life pass on and new life emerge. Nature could also end each life with a swift cut – the kind of death many dream of, but one destined to elude most, for nature prefers the slow process of senescence. This way sufficient time remains to tend to young, budding life, to share one's experiences and continue gathering new ones. Living by this *natural* sense of aging means, metaphorically speaking, going on flourishing for one's own and others' sake for as long as it may be given to a more or less indestructible plant, and consenting to the inevitable onset of wilting. It means celebrating life – all life, including one's own – for as long as it lasts, and beyond; it means experiencing life's plenitude and accepting its temporal limits with gelassenheit. Are we capable of that?

A *cultural* sense of aging might consist in the discovery of resources that will enrich and alleviate our life in this stage in particular. Gelassenheit is one such resource. There seems to be a shortage of it these days. The modern world makes us restless, casting our lives in such turmoil as to make us long for gelassenheit. An important topic in Western philosophy and Christian theology going back to Epicurus' (341-270 B.C.E.) notion of *ataraxia* and Meister Eckhart's (c.1260-c.1328) concept of *gelazenheit*, it has been forgotten in modern times, having fallen prey to militant activism and scientific-technological optimism. Its gentle reserve is no longer rated a virtue; yet, the would-be *coolness* that has come to replace it still retains the memory of its human warmth. For centuries, one life stage in particular appeared to have been made for gelassenheit: old age. But it, too, has now become a time of upheaval – gelassenheit doesn't seem to be able to succeed as easily anymore. How can it be regained? Can a society that is growing increasingly older grow more gelassen as well?

I don't possess gelassenheit, but for me it is something I ought to aspire to if I wish to live a beautiful life. It is certainly a gift in any life stage, but it is particularly beneficial as we get on in years, as life gets harder and more scant. It may actually be the case that gelassenheit only becomes possible as we grow older. After all, it is easier to be gelassen when no longer everything is at stake, when our hormones are no longer raging, when we have a lifetime's worth of experience, a broadened outlook and a time-tested sense for people and things to rely on.

This book outlines ten steps to gelassenheit based on observation, experience and reflection. It is about the kind of gelassenheit that is itself gelassen, and not at all boastful and provocative ("Look at me and how gelassen I am!"). And it is about staking out, together with the reader, a sensible and practi-

cal path that will actually lead to gelassenheit, rather than simply proclaiming it. The
first step on this journey consists in the willingness to reflect on the stages of life, which
never stands still, and to gain an understanding of the idiosyncrasies of aging and old age
so as to be open to them.

1
THOUGHTS ON THE STAGES
OF LIFE

❧

What actually is life? Something intensely
palpable, then again not; ostensibly always
the same, then again ever-changing; full of
variety at times, then again mundane and
repetitive. It brings desire and happiness, and
also pain and misfortune, and no one knows
how this allotment works. It makes us long
for intimacy and relationships, which we

then flee, and it calls for mindfulness, only to have us mindlessly drift on again. *Polarity* is a core feature of life. It oscillates between opposite poles such as anger and joy, fear and hope, longing and disappointment, becoming and passing, which were long accepted as ineluctable fate. Constantly something is born while something else passes on. Every becoming goes hand in hand with a passing, and every passing with a becoming, and the same goes for the becoming that is aging. In modern times, however, living with this polarity has become questionable. How can we learn to face it with gelassenheit?

It helps to be mindful of the different stages of life if we wish to do justice to the particulars of each. They seem to resemble the different times of day: some of us get up and hit the ground running, while others are not morning persons at all; still, in this stage, we often cannot wait for the day to begin. With infinite time and endless possibilities on our hands, in the prime of life we enjoy the challenge of rising to the occasion and getting on with our work, accomplishing the day's business with ease, until, unawares, we suddenly find ourselves on lunch break. Then it is already afternoon, which can drag on forever. We become sluggish, feel a bit drained, and a gaping void opens up unexpectedly. How to get through it? The day's nadir is punctured by the sudden realization that it is drawing to a close and that there is still so much to do. But – no need to panic, we will have plenty of time after dinner. After dinner, however, it is more important to catch up with family, friends and acquaintances, until we are exhausted and ready to turn in.

Similarly with the stages of life, even though they may unfold quite differently for each of us (and may need to be parsed more subtly and in greater detail). Acknowledging them, giving them the time and attention they deserve (and will claim anyway) is the first step to gelassenheit. The *first quarter of life* corresponds to the early morning. And although getting up may be a pain, our first few decades seem rife with infinite possibility: we can be anything, we feel immortal in the boundless space of possibility, and it is up to us to explore it through play, trial and error, and education. We are energized by what appears to be an endlessly open horizon, it is a time of pure *possibility* and *potential* 'know-how': in this life stage "I can do this" means "I could, if I only wanted to."

From the start, however, our life is prone to aging – almost imperceptibly at first, and then in spurts that can take us by surprise and be quite difficult to manage. It begins in the womb without our noticing it; then, at three, we cannot wait to be six, and at six we want nothing more than to be twelve, and at twelve we are dying to be eighteen. As we put the turmoils of puberty behind us, we begin experiencing the passage of time in a new way. The years that dragged on forever for the child zoom by for the adult, and there is barely any time or space left for gelassenheit. By that point, some of us know exactly what they want and rush to get ahead; others are still searching and would prefer making a U-turn: "I'm scared of getting old," a twenty-year-old tells me. Sometimes, puberty seamlessly transitions into a serious existential crisis, early disappointments in relationships and failed projects can lead to a so-called *quarter-life crisis*.

A lot happens in the first quarter. It is a period of virtually endless experimentation, and the experiences we gather in this life stage will come in handy later in life. The transition to the *second quarter of life* occurs on the fly, and it is only in the late morning, around our thirtieth birthday, that the suspicion creeps in that, contrary to appearances, the horizon will not remain open forever. And while this intimation cannot be pinned down to a specific year or date in our life – the range tends to be pretty wide here – for the first time we find ourselves asking: which of our projects are still realistic?

Time is of the essence when it comes to getting on with long-term projects such as starting a family or reaching career goals.

These external pressures, however, tend to be dwarfed by the pressure we put on ourselves to finally commit to the decisions we have made and to seriously work on realizing our ideas and goals in our relationships with others, ourselves and the world at large – so long as we wish to accomplish anything at all. Saying good-bye to the conditional ("I could if I only wanted to") is the hallmark of this life stage. Now is the time to prove our mettle and to show the world what we can really do. "I can do this" now means actually making it happen, if need be over the long haul and against major obstacles. Sheer excitement about the tasks at hand trumps any doubts we may have about being able to rise to the challenge. Our profound sense of being firmly grounded in life, powerful and invincible (even if occasionally stressed out), makes it easy to forget that we are getting older.

Somewhere between forty and fifty, then, and in full swing, we cross the noon meridian, the midpoint of our life (assuming our life expectancy to be eighty, ninety or a hundred, which is not at all improbable in contemporary first-world societies). From now on, the number of years left will always be smaller than the number of years gone by. Aging is ever on our heels, like a stalker who does not keep a safety distance and cannot even be indicted for it. Getting body, mind and spirit naturally in tune with this new life stage may be rough sailing – not unlike the storms of puberty – and may drag on for years. At a time when, following a sumptuous midday meal, we feel full with life and a bit sluggish, this may come as a shock. At such a time, gelassenheit is probably only possible if we are truly willing to trust the process and simply let aging happen.

Midlife crisis and *menopause* completely change our perspective on life: up to this point it was *prospective*, open-ended and future-oriented ("What will my life be like? What do I want to achieve, and what can I do to get there?"); now it becomes *retrospective*, tapering off toward the front and getting progressively rear-heavy ("What has my life been like? What have I created and accomplished?")

When we were young, we were not at all interested in contemplating or talking about aging, dying and death; now, conversely, we cannot help thinking about these issues, unless we consciously work on suppressing them. As we enter this new life stage, with its unique physical and spiritual characteristics, our outlook changes accordingly. All of us are anchored in our individual viewpoints, which are subject to the influences of our unique situations, work environments, experiences and relationships. So dominant is each individual perspective, in fact, that assuming someone else's is almost inconceivable; and even though it may at times be possible to empathize with or mentally put ourselves in another's place – an older or younger person's, for instance – this new 'adopted perspective' will never truly become ours. Thus, our newly gained, 'broader' midlife perspective, too, which may appear to have overcome the limitations of youth, will perforce necessarily be limited: to our own current life situation. And so, even as our overall understanding of life's finitude ostensibly increases with age, it cannot but remain fairly theoretical given that the end of life is still something that is looming in the distant future.

2

UNDERSTANDING THE IDIOSYNCRASIES OF AGING

As we get older, the second step to Gelassenheit consists in learning as much as we can about the idiosyncrasies of this life stage, in being open to whatever it may bring, especially its challenges. The *third quarter of life* holds the promise of years – maybe even decades – of activity made all the more joyful and rewarding by our realization that the possibilities still open to us are steadily decreasing in number. As we get older, we witness the fount of our possibilities drying up. And so, with all our might we begin to protest: this can't have been it! Some think they can salvage their dwindling options by abandoning ongoing projects and ending existing relationships in order to start over one last time.

Life's afternoon, too, has its particular kind of *'expert know-how'*. Now, more than ever before, "I can do this" means: I know how the world works, and I can do the familiar routines in my sleep. This way, I can compensate for being past my prime (compensation). In fact, my mental abilities seem to have increased, for I can direct and focus them much better now (concentration). I no longer have to try my hand at everything; instead, I can prioritize and be more judicious in my choices (selection). And whatever I do, I can do it expertly and reliably (optimization). This fourfold 'know-how' (compensa-

tion, concentration, selection, optimization)
is a matter of intuition, which is the result of
years and years of experience – both good
and bad – and which we can continue fine-
tuning. Acquiring new skills can certainly
complement experience, but it can never replace it. In the business world, companies
would do well to draw on their older em-
ployees' wealth of experience, which they
will be happy to share with their younger
colleagues. In an ideal world, the younger
generation's bustling creativity will be wed
to their elders' circumspect prudence. If this
could succeed across society, then this might
help to cool down our overheated modern
world and bring about a different kind of
modernity.

The superior 'know-how' of the third
quarter of life should not only affect everything related to work but all areas of life, particularly the way we treat ourselves and
others. Shouldn't we hope that with age we
might become 'masters of living', as the me-
dieval mystic Meister Eckhart was nick-

named? Wouldn't this constitute life's very fulfillment and the true purpose of the art of living? But only those who have completed their apprenticeship accede to mastery, which is why there cannot be perfect mastery when it comes to the art of living. To the very last, life remains a learning project. We never cease having to take on board new experiences and new challenges, social shifts and technological advances. This kind of knowledge, as we well know, can never reach the point of indubitable certainty. Already the Stoic philosopher Seneca observed: "It takes a lifetime to learn how to live."

What we now have to accept are the visible signs of aging. Being a friend to oneself in this life stage means befriending the disconcerting symptoms of senescence that begin to show. In the course of the third quarter, aging is particularly noticeable in others – but what about ourselves? Our hair begins to thin and gray, the lines in our face become more pronounced, our ailments become more frequent. Our body starts feeling rusty if we don't work it out. And even though it may be a blessing to be able to alleviate the painful side effects of aging, doggedly fighting the process only deepens the lines in the warrior's face. Forming new relationships gets harder, which is why we appreciate the intimacy and familiarity of existing bonds all the more and cultivate our friendships with greater care and attention. The emotional storms of the past have blown over, life flows gently along, to the point of occasional boredom: been there, done this, nothing new under the sun.

As we turn sixty, then, we are startled into the realization that life's afternoon will soon be over and that it might be wise not to put everything off until the evening. The *immortality bubble* inside which we have felt safe and secure for the longest time, and which has of late started showing the occasional crack, has now irrevocably popped. Now we know our life's possibilities: we have lived them. For many years, they lay before us shrouded in fog, only gradually coming into view. Now many of them lie behind us, and we live the reality they have accrued with or without our doing. Should there be further possibilities left, now is our last chance to realize them. Certain questions become more pressing then ever: what do I want to hold on to? which doors are still open? what do I still need to do? what is important to me, and what should I no longer put off? should I completely upend my life one last time and be stressed out again? how much time do I have left? which projects are still feasible? how can I make sure that I understand a world that is so rapidly changing? do I have enough strength left for all that? and if so, for how long?

Now gelassenheit means befriending the inconspicuous little word 'still'. Its increasing frequency in our lives unmistakably points to the accelerating process of aging: "You *still* look good for your age!" "How fit you *still* are!" "How impressive that you can *still* do the math in your head!" "How bold of you to *still* be dressing like a young man!" "Are you *still* doing okay?" The key is not to get upset about these and similar remarks, they mean no harm; on the contrary, they are supposed to comfort, uplift and encourage. Besides, the simple truth is that even though what these remarks speak to may *still* be the case, it won't be the case for long. In this life stage, 'still' reigns supreme. We can *still* call a friend and chat with him, we can *still* offer an apology we feel we owe, we can *still* return a favor and say thank you for whatever and to whomever.

More and more frequently, we think back to the past and recall missed opportunities and painful losses, momentous encounters and opportunities taken, key situations and memorable experiences that shine more brightly now that the present appears to be growing darker. The realization that we are not as strong as we used to be might lead us to believe that life boils down to a gradual loss of strength. Yet forcing our body, mind and spirit in this stage to accomplish tasks that no longer come easy will only accelerate

41

the depletion of whatever resources we have left. Certainly, every once in a while things will be looking up again, even over extended periods. On the whole, though, it will be more like the story of the mouse that got caught by a cat: "Things are looking up," says the mouse as it is being dragged up the stairs and into the house.

This stage can last a long time. In affluent societies, for more people than ever before the third quarter does not at all mean the beginning of the end. For it is followed by a *fourth quarter*, which used to be but the tail end of the third: now, however, we transition from an *agile* to a *fragile*, accelerated senescence, which typically sets in somewhere between seventy-five and eighty. A chasm opens up between those who must now live with major disabilities and those whose radiance reaches its peak. One way or another, however, there comes a point when our abilities begin to erode, either seamlessly, or abruptly and painfully. Should we really embark on new projects *now*? It's over. Our versatility wanes, our possibilities plummet, until eventually only the last one is left – before disappearing in turn, even though this may take a while. What we may have once poetically imagined as the 'evening of our lives' may turn out to be a fairly prosaic affair due to all sorts of disability. Mastering them will be a challenge, as modern culture does not prepare us for them.

Now we ought to learn to slow down, to budget our resources, to be more considerate toward ourselves, perhaps to spend more time alone than we used to, review our lives and acknowledge death, which no longer looms in the distant future. Aging brings hardships that the young cannot possibly know anything about, such as finding one's way through the increasingly complex mazes of the latest technology, or overcoming as simple an obstacle as getting in and out of the bathtub, which we used to be able to do with ease.

Again, just as in infancy, *mobility* becomes our top priority. However, in contrast to the child's triumphant experience of standing up, learning to walk and gaining independence in the process – literally, step by step – we find ourselves bent over by age, sometimes no longer able to move from one place to another at will. Gravity, which we once proudly stood up to, mercilessly pulls us downward. Reduced mobility goes hand in hand with reduced reaction time. And sooner or later we have to decide when to hand in our driver's license. Even the smallest goodbye may be difficult, for in it we glimpse the final farewell.

All of us, including those who 'have stayed young', grow old. And so it would be wise early on to find or create appropriate spaces for aging, to imagine what it will feel like, to ask ourselves what needs we will have and what kinds of environment we would like to grow old in. In our own home, with ambulatory care, if need be? Surrounded by our family and with the help of a nurse? With others who are in a similar situation? In a multi-generational home? In an assisted-living community? How much will all this cost? How can we ensure that all the necessary arrangements be made in time? Which spaces are already equipped for the particular needs of the elderly? Whom should we entrust with helping us to let go of our much-cherished independence, which we may lose against our will as we get older?

It is not really up to us to decide how we will grow older, least of all in the fourth quarter. No one has ever chosen to have porous bones, or to become depressed or demented. No one wants to be bent over or wizened, and yet these things happen. Our body no longer regenerates; it degenerates. For good reason, then, the modern age saw the creation of homes for the elderly, who can no longer keep up: in order to protect them from the young, who will trample them, and the machines that will crush them – and, last but not least (and more bleakly), in order to retire them and no longer have to take them into account. I myself tend to impatiently hurry past the elderly on the street, they are simply too slow for a 'junior senior' like me. I know, it is totally unfair and not gelassen of me at all to have no patience with this kind of pokiness. They stop every couple of feet to catch their breath, and I think to myself: God, they are really old, much older than I, and I simply cannot imagine that before long I will be one of them.

But I have also noticed of late that I have taken to keeping my hand close to the banister when walking up and down stairs, on the off chance that I might trip and need to hold on to something, for I know full well that I would not be able to handle a misstep as smoothly and elegantly as I used to; or that I fumble in my pockets for keys that I never put there. My senses, too, once so keen and alert, have gradually been going downhill: I now have to hold the newspaper at arm's length if I want to be able to read it. After all, I would not want anyone to catch me wearing glasses (which I need a little more time to get used to). And when someone is talking to me, I discreetly turn my good ear toward them. A hearing aid? Never! I don't mind no longer hearing everything – in fact, it is a relief not to have to respond to everything all the time. What is annoying, though, is the impatience of those around me, who begrudge me this newfound freedom.

Aging, as caregivers well know, can take extreme forms: in childhood we transition from being completely dependent on and cared for by others to gradually learning to take care of ourselves; in old age, conversely, we transition from taking care of ourselves to being cared for by others. In many respects, as we grow old we go through infancy and childhood again, only in reverse. We grow out of diapers and eventually grow back into them, needing to be fed, put to bed, wheeled around – not all of us, of course, but a good many for sure. Our sense of time and space, acquired in early childhood, atrophies toward the end of our lives. What once was easy gets hard as we gradually lose whatever strength we have left. Cherished habits can be of great help during this process, and those who can fall back on them can count themselves truly lucky! Having our habits do the work for us makes for gelassenheit.

3

HABITS MAKE LIFE EASIER

No doubt, it would be great if life in the fourth quarter never needed to be uprooted, if it were always allowed to remain in the soil of its long-standing habits. After all, changing one's lifestyle can be a formidable enough challenge in the third quarter already. And although we can get used to virtually anything (even pain, as long as it is not too intense), this takes time – and strength – both of which we may no longer have as we get on in years. The whole point of habit is to allow us to comfortably and effortlessly follow its lead: cultivating our habits, then, is the third step to Gelassenheit. The elderly cling to their habits because they depend on them and so as not to have to constantly reinvent their lives. Unfortunately, they are often incapable of breaking even those habits that are not good for them and put others off. Or has it always been like that?

Habits are an integral part of how we live, and the only thing that stands in the way of their being recognized as a core component of any lifestyle is that in the modern age they have fallen into disrepute. Habits are boring, right? And boredom is modernity's archenemy: monotonous, devoid of variety and novelty. But the elderly are not the only ones negatively affected by modernity's habit-phobia. Everyone knows from their own experience how good it feels every once in a while to be able to safely fall back on the familiar, to retreat from the onslaught of unexpected challenges into the comfort of a pair of old slacks. Habits are soothing because they are repetitive and reliable.

Which is why the art of living also involves the conscious formation of habits, so as to be guided by everything that has already been decided in them. Life rolls along gently and predictably on the tracks of habit, which endows it with a necessity that cannot easily be undone. Whether voluntarily set in motion or involuntarily shuffling along, my feet find their usual destinations on their own; breakfast finds its way into my mouth virtually without my doing while I scan the morning paper; my hand reaches for the shelf at the grocery store automatically and without my putting any thought into it (unless the food items have been rearranged); every Saturday morning my favorite radio show lifts me up, and at my regular café I no longer need to order the usual before delving into world affairs with the waiter; dinner, too, virtually prepares itself as long as I don't have to think about each individual step.

Whoever doubts the importance of habit for the everyday should conduct the following experiment: choose one day that you will spend completely habit-free – a Sunday, for instance – a day on which the consequences of your experiment won't do too much damage. On this day, as soon as you wake up, everything you do will be a matter of deciding what to do. The problem is: how will you ever get out of bed? After all, this first action of the day requires several steps of serious deliberation: why? what for? with which foot first? and at what time exactly? This can take hours, and should you finally find yourself in the vertical position, the process continues: why go to the bathroom (after all, that's only a ritual)? and what to have for breakfast? tea or coffee, or something else? Whatever you are used to is off limits, and as soon as you have dealt with this embarrassment of riches you cannot decide which mug to use, for you have twenty to choose from and you cannot use the beat-up one that you like best, for using it would mean yielding to habit, and that is precisely what is in question.

We moderns do not like to admit it, but habits afford us a welcome time-out from the countless decisions we would otherwise constantly have to make. Only if a good chunk of our day transpires without our thinking about it, and as if on its own, are those energies set free that enable us to properly deal with all the other chunks that fall outside the norm. Now, whatever does not get caught in the safety net of habit can receive proper attention, those decisions in particular that do not need to be made every day. Which does not mean that these decisions, too, will not in turn benefit from our habitual judgment patterns, for more often than not when we need to make a decision our mind is filled with chaos rather than clarity. In order to be able to make sensible decisions in any given situation, we would do well to gain a good understanding of its human and non-human elements. And, lest we get lost in the muddle of the unfamiliar, there is no better way to learn these things than to be dealing with them hands-on over and over again until they become part of our routine.

The significance of habit goes much deeper, however: it is precisely this braided yarn of context and routine that effortlessly weaves us into a fabric of *meaning* without our having to constantly do the work ourselves. We arrange our lives in the shelter of habit, and this process of getting-used-to generates the familiarity with our environment that constitutes the essence of *home*. It is not on account of its four walls that a place becomes a home, but owing to all the habits and routines that form in and around it. Both a new apartment and a vacation home have four walls, yet neither feels like home, which is the child of habit. And as soon as a place becomes a home, leaving it will be hard. The history of humanity as well as our own individual histories poignantly testify to just how much we depend on the protective shelter of habit: think of all the situations when in the midst of crisis or tragedy we keep up the routines that give our life rhythm, from which it can draw strength again.

Be it inside or outside the home, habits puncture the unfamiliar and create familiarity. This applies to behavioral patterns, habits of seeing, hearing, thinking and feeling, as well as the shared routines and rituals of a relationship. Even problems depend on routines. Thus, we do not necessarily wish to get rid of those problems that we have gotten used to and that have become life fixtures: why fix something if it isn't broken? In fact, as we get older, we find ourselves wanting to preserve our lives just as they are and despite the problems this may cause. We are afraid of getting lost in case we fail. Much less than the young do we trust in the power of new habits to recreate the sense of familiarity and home provided by our old habits.

This might entail a certain reverence for habit, insofar as it enables us to more easily inhabit the spaces and behaviors, thoughts and opinions, emotions and problems that make up our lives. Of course, it would be desirable if every once in a while we could break some of our habits rather than holing up in them; but this does not change the fact that we typically hand over up to three quarters of our existence to them. The young are able to keep the share of habit in their lives fairly low; the older we get, however, the more our lives become entrenched in habit, and the more uprooted we feel when we have to leave a familiar environment, lose an old acquaintance, or when a relationship we have grown used to ends. And should change be inevitable, then we need to make sure, if at all possible, to preserve at least some of our routines. The enjoyment of bodily pleasures, too, nurtured and cultivated over time, can be secured through habit – fortunately, even as we grow older.

4
ENJOYING BODILY PLEASURES AND HAPPINESS

As if to compensate for all its potential ills, aging is accompanied by the pleasant sense of a certain lightness of being. Consciously enjoying bodily pleasures, and experiencing happiness that way, constitutes the fourth step to gelassenheit. More than ever before we welcome those *humble pleasures* that dare to surface now that the storms of passion have blown over. Knowing that we will not be able to enjoy them indefinitely makes them all the more precious, even though we do not exactly know when we will hear the blackbird's warble in the early spring for the last time, or smell the freshly-mown grass in the balmy summer night air, or shuffle through the wilting autumn leaves on the ground, or enjoy the cozy warmth indoors while feasting our eyes on the thick snow flakes outside.

Not to mention a good cup of espresso, which warms the body and inspires the mind. What goes for wine goes for coffee, too: life is too short to have the bad kind. The scent of the light-brown *crema*, the taste of the pitch-black brew, the stimulating effect of caffeine are all pleasures that alone warrant mourning life's gradual decline and hoping that it may last a good while. But there is no need to get depressed over having to reduce the amount of coffee with age. Each and every grain tastes all the more delicious now, whereas in the past huge quantities

used to avalanche down our gullets to no noticeable effect. Gelassenheit means being
pervaded by this kind of enjoyment. It is precisely this *conscious ability* to experience joy
that is one of the main reasons for "accepting
and loving" old age, as Seneca puts it in his
Moral Epistles, for "it is full of pleasures, so
long as we know how to enjoy them."

In my own case, I have noticed for instance that not only has my love of good coffee been steadily growing, but my *wanderlust*,
too. Does this suggest a renewed hunger for
life? The less time I have left, the more destinations come to mind. *1,000 Places to See
Before You Die* goes the title of a popular book;
but even a cursory tally tells me that visiting
all the one thousand places to see before you
die will no longer be possible – unless I don't
mind both the expense and the stress of constantly being on the road, as well as the risk
of depleting both my finances and myself, as
I have seen it happen to others: "Soon we'll
be out of places to go," an octogenarian (and
frequent cruise ship passenger) once told me

in passing on a train. Could it be that he had nothing left, least of all something to look forward to beyond his own life? Still, he was doughtily going to plod on: "What should we save our money for? Our children? They should earn their own keep!"

The *joys of remembering*, in particular, which played a minor role when we were still looking ahead, increase exponentially as we grow older and reach the age of retrospection. We enjoy looking back and surveying all our experiences and achievements. Reveling in memories is all the more gratifying now that we no longer have to suffer the uncertainty of how our story will end, for the ending is well known. Even melancholy reminiscences we may now experience as pleasant and sweet rather than painful and bitter – think of Carol King's 1966 song *Going Back*, which often gets covered by aging pop stars, such as Phil Collins. It is nice to indulge in nostalgia at the sound of music, which may revive feelings of the distant past, when our lives were still fresh: countless radio stations bank on the power of oldies that leave their listeners with the sadness of a world gone by – a world that may feel like it was the best of possible worlds, while the present seems to be taking them ever farther away from the 'true' life.

Now we can reap the benefits of having started working on the memories of the future early on. For what once was the future is the present now, and what once was the present has now receded into the past. Proudly I think back to all the risky ventures that I pulled off and that outshine the ones that failed. I was – I am – all that. But is any of it true? Each memory dredges up the internal sediments of the past. Yet we have to keep in mind that sometimes our memories of the many narratives that make up our biographies are fictions designed to weave the tangled strands of our lives into a coherent narrative fabric that makes sense. When someone listens, we are inspired to tell stories, to tweak and embellish them. In life's warm evening glow everything acquires a softer hue, and the distance in time creates the impression of spatial distance as well, which allows us to view the events of the past like a tapestry on the horizon of our existence, palpably mingling reality, in all its plasticity, with the artifices of the imagination.

One particular joy, which grows ever more intense with age, is the *joy of conversation*, perhaps even the joy of writing things down for oneself and others. We have a lot more time on our hands and an endless string of experiences and reflections that clamor for expression and being shared with others. Like the evening sky at dusk, this is life's *blue hour*, which inspires us to find a comfortable nook to talk to each other and share thoughts and events. If only we could take turns talking! If only we could avoid bending the others' ear with things we have already told them, and ask ourselves instead whether now wouldn't be a good time to pull out the stories we haven't told yet, provided there is interest. This way, all the things we may have been holding back and that may have been a secret burden can finally come out. But conversation fails when there is nobody who will listen, and that seems to be a real problem in old age: for the many who have something to share there is only a handful who are willing to listen. Storytelling groups or meet-ups that require taking turns sharing and listening may be the solution to this problem.

And what about sex in old age? It keeps us young. Since it has broken into mainstream film culture, we no longer think of old people having sex as gross or off-putting. If no one among the aging would have previously admitted to wanting it, now it has virtually become a profession of faith. But our *libido* changes with age: the lengths we used to go to to placate our raging hormones is something we no longer quite understand, jumping each other doesn't happen that often anymore. Yet the reduced frequency of intercourse facilitates increased intensity. Now, post-coital exhaustion may have other reasons than in the past, our heart and circulation could now be in serious danger. At least we no longer have to fear the *one-night-stand burnout* that sometimes afflicts the young. There simply aren't enough willing partners. Unplanned procreation is improbable, which means that sex could finally be purely a medium of communication, inspiration and exultation. More and more, though, conversation takes over that role. Our waning potency can be elegantly glossed over: "I'm just not interested in it anymore!" Certainly, there are pills that will reignite desire, but do we really want this if it doesn't happen on its own? Does our partner want this? That is something to discuss. Here, gelassenheit will consist in light-heartedly letting go of something that has seemed so important throughout our lives. Sex becoming less important may even contribute to more relaxed friendships between the sexes.

Many feel an increased *desire for gardening* with age. Digging into the loam with both hands changes a person. In the garden, time spins in circles, which dovetails with our overall experience of time as we age: we feel closer to earth's cyclical time than to the linear time of modernity. In the garden, we feel that human existence, too, is firmly rooted in the order of nature, where finitude affects the part but not the whole. Why do humans love gardens? Because, like religion, they are balm for the wound of mortality, which has pained humanity since time immemorial. We moderns have a particularly difficult time with finitude, since we think that we will fall into a black hole at the end of our journey (all the while believing that this is not a form of faith). Gardens suggest that recycling, being reintegrated into the cycles of nature, is possible at the level of the individual as well. The small plot of land in our backyard stands for the cycle of death and rebirth, which is also our fate, beyond our finitude. But how to imagine this?

Now is a good time to reflect on life – something we may have put off all our lives. We can yield to the *desire for leisure*, engage in purposeless activities and simply *be*. Like children, we can devote ourselves to the things that interest and fascinate us; freedom of thought makes for the most interesting connections. *Carpe diem*, seize and savor the day: now is the time to live by this maxim, but also to understand that this doesn't mean savoring *every day*. For there are less enjoyable days that are still good for something: they make the enjoyable ones even more precious. Gelassenheit does not require that everything give pleasure. Far from it, it is the great privilege of the gelassenheit of aging that we no longer feel we have to chase every desire that comes our way; and "what we find instead of our desires," as Seneca writes, "is the desire not to desire."

Ongoing *activity* can now be enriched by *passivity*, which has acquired such a bad reputation in the modern age. The art of living presents the following options for life lived the gelassen way: we can remain *active* and socially engaged, stay in shape and continue learning new things; or we can become *pas-*

sive and withdraw from society – our only activity consisting in taking care of ourselves and being there for family and friends. Those who wish to save the aging from calcification through 'activity therapies' certainly mean well, but this kind of strategy rather bespeaks a certain helplessness and lack of imagination on modernity's part. When else, if not in old age, can we claim the universal right to be passive? After all, life itself pushes us to accept with gelassenheit much of what cannot be changed, especially when it comes to experiencing pain and tragedy.

5

DEALING WITH PAIN
AND TRAGEDY

❧

What we need as we grow older? Health, to be sure. For the longest time we took it for granted. Now it becomes a project. We can do a lot for our health, take proper care of ourselves, eat healthily, exercise and surround ourselves with people and things that are good for us. But only few of us manage to stay healthy to the very last. The probability of pain and illness does not decrease with age. We can attempt to put up a protective wall of desire around us, harness positive experiences to seal ourselves off against the negative. Yet the fifth step to gelassenheit consists precisely in our heightened capacity for acceptance when confronted with both the minor and major ills of aging. How to get there?

I am plagued by back pain and a stiff neck. Why? How do I get rid of this? And what else is in the offing? In the morning, I drag myself to the bathroom, the way I used to ages ago after pulling an all-nighter. I feel completely drained, and all my bones ache. Is this what it is going to be like from now on? The age spots on my skin do not hurt physically, but they do hurt my aesthetic sensibilities. It also hurts that I can no longer work all night the way I used to. "Your gums have been receding faster," my dentist regretfully tells me – which certainly isn't good news for my teeth and, consequently, for me as a whole. "Arthritis," my GP observes – "but only the beginning stages," he quickly adds. For the longest time, 'prostate' was one of those nondescript foreign terms to me, now I know a whole lot more about it. Sometimes I feel dizzy getting out of bed, what does this mean? And doesn't my heart skip a beat every once in a while?

All right, that is a bit exaggerated, but I would rather be a hypochondriac than an ignoramus, for this way I will stay alert. And since it will hardly get any better, I want to at least be prepared for it. The *nocebo effect* — that I might actually experience the negative symptoms of whatever I am afraid of — does not really bother me; I am much more apprehensive about the *'no-response effect'* — about not having the strength and courage to face the negative when it comes.

Should living with pain become unavoidable, there is a range of possible *interventions*, and their existence is quite reassuring: pharmaceutical, therapeutic, meditational, surgical — all subtly calibrated to our individual needs and situations. What is equally impor-

tant to consider, though, is how to produc-
tively *integrate* pain into our daily lives – a
question of particular significance when it
comes to chronic pain. After all, we do not
want to waste all our energy on a battle we
cannot realistically hope to win.

Pain has an enormous impact on our
lives, it hits the modern ego where it is most
vulnerable: in its claim to autonomy and independence. The gelassenheit of independence, however, can also mean accepting pain,
within limits, and it is up to us to decide up
to which point, if need be in consultation
with a physician. What for? So as to experience life in its very depth for as long as we
can possibly endure it; so as not to fret and
waver every time pain, illness or tragedy hit,
but instead to befriend whatever happens to
and with us and, possibly, make it our own.
The great advantage of this kind of possession is that nobody will envy us for it, that it
will be wholly and completely ours.

Many things in life depend on luck, both
good and bad, and no one really knows why

it is one or the other in any given case. There
is no point in reproaching oneself, others or
life in general whenever something that
shouldn't happen happens. Tragedies do oc-
cur, illnesses do exist, certainties do get shak-
en. Why me? There is no real answer here.
Why me now? It could be pure chance.
When will I be rid of it again? Maybe never.
And what then? Then I can only hope that I
will know how to adequately deal with it, for
instance by saying to myself: this is the task
that life has now put before me – be it by
chance or necessity. I accept this challenge in
order to turn it into something positive, for
it must be good for something. Is all that happens ultimately good for something? Not
necessarily for a predetermined good, not always for the affected, and sometimes only in
hindsight. In the fullness of time, and often
beyond an individual's lifespan, what seemed
incomprehensible at first may in a later context suddenly make sense and gain significance (which it may have contained all
along).

It is fundamentally beyond our control to turn off the polarity of life, the tension between the positive and the negative. There is no life without it, as our ancestors well knew and as sun dials still teach us: light and shadow go together. Modernity's faith in a happy here and now, however, entails the expectation of being able to ban the negative from life entirely, in conspicuous analogy to the religious belief in a happy hereafter, in which only the paradisiacal state of the purely positive obtains. Given the prospect of an afterlife, phenomena such as existential doubt, negative thinking and melancholy had no place in the Christian world for centuries on end, and were denounced as deadly sins.

The deadly sin of the modern age, however, is depression: something that has always been part and parcel of humanity, an *anthropological constant* – being depressed, downcast or unhappy – is suddenly viewed as a serious transgression, and branded an 'illness' in our post-moral age. Yet, in fact, many of those who think they suffer from depression and have been diagnosed as such are really *melancholy*. They merely have the *blues* – to use a colloquialism – which is nothing but good old melancholy, a state of the soul that should not be considered pathological. Contrary to the root meaning of 'melancholy' ('black bile' in ancient Greek), there doesn't necessarily have to be anything bitter about it.

As we get older, we tend to suffer from it more than the young. This equally applies to the actual illness of *depression*, which, in contrast to the emotional and intellectual agitations of melancholy, is characterized by atrophied feelings and a general incapacity for reflection. The truly depressed person can no longer help himself or escape the narrow compass of his own thoughts, having to rely on relatives and friends to be there for him, on therapists and doctors to treat him.

Which is not to say that distinguishing between melancholy and full-blown depression is easy, there is a gray area here. However, the fact that these days melancholy gets more and more frequently diagnosed as depression drives the numbers of patients to absurd proportions. This is good for the pharmaceutical industry and for improving public awareness of the illness, but not for our dealings with the individual. Thus, a person who is in the grip of melancholy doesn't really need medication as a first line of treatment but someone to talk to; whereas a person who is clinically depressed needs a doctor and a proper course of treatment.

Melancholy comes uninvited and can have many reasons. Loss of certainty can cause sadness, which may not easily be relieved. People fall into depression if they lose something important to them, but also if they don't win or get something they had hoped for. And even in moments when a long-nurtured wish has finally been fulfilled an unexpected void may open up: for a long time, working toward a goal had given life meaning and direction; no sooner has the goal been reached, however, than we no longer have something to focus on. This may be one of the, often underestimated, dangers of fixating on the far-away goal of retirement.

But there are also out-and-out times of melancholy: in the fall, when the leaves fall, in the winter when the sun "will not show his head," or when we happen to experience a *quarter-life*, *midlife* or other kind of *crisis* triggered by memories of happier times. Whether melancholy will be a fleeting visitor or whether it has come to stay is not always immediately clear. Often, it will pass on its own if we simply accept it, let it come and go with gelassenheit. But this has nothing to do with 'overcoming' it, there is no such mandate. Much more adequate is the notion that this aspect of being human, too, serves to enrich and complete our overall experience of life.

What makes us melancholy with age, above all, is the experience of an *existential loneliness*, which is exacerbated in a culture that more than any other adulates the ego. Meanwhile, the ego is thrown back upon itself with a vengeance: *I* live this life, no one else. *I* have to endure peering into the gaping

abyss opened up before me by my own unhappiness or a tragic event. Only *I* can ultimately live this life to the end, no one else
can do it for me. And how *I* think about the
hereafter is different from how others think
about it. Incomprehensible is the pain of
weltschmerz that I feel about the human con-
dition and the world as whole. Extremely
painful is the conscious acceptance of the
fact that my life will end, that one day I will
have to leave this life and the ones I love, that
this moment is inexorably approaching and
no longer a point in the remote future.

"Where are we now?" David Bowie asks
in his 2013 song with such a twinge of
melancholy in his voice that many radio stations stopped playing it despite its initial success: they did not think they could burden
their listeners with so much sadness. In a
handful of lines Bowie reminisces about
Berlin, where he lived from 1976 to 1978.
And now, at sixty-six, he realizes that all he
does is "just walking the dead." Nothing lasts,

all things must pass, and the past cannot be brought back, "you know, you know." That all things must pass, even though the new never ceases coming to pass, cannot be changed. That is something that preoccupies us more than ever before as we age. But so as not to be too hard on ourselves, we ought to avail ourselves of the many forms of touch, which make it easier to muster gelassenheit, particularly in difficult times.

6
EXPERIENCING INTIMACY THROUGH TOUCH

Throughout our lives, we depend on touching and being touched. From the moment we are born, touch is a core element in the building and strengthening of our immune system, in creating human bonds and feeling sheltered. As children in particular, we feel comforted in another's arms. But as adults, too, we know the soothing power of the touch of a hand. A racing pulse can be calmed, high blood pressure lowered by the warm proximity of another person. Seeking touch is the sixth step to gelassenheit.

It is often through touch that people get to know each other: a casual touch of another's arm immediately creates a situation of trust, and the further touch is allowed to go, the more intimate the relationship between two people will become. Conversely, if we wish to distance ourselves from another person, we stop touching them and do not allow them to touch us. This experience is deeply ingrained in the fabric of our existence. When I am being touched, I am alive and feel that I am alive. When I am no longer touched, life eludes me, I no longer feel it. Touch is a form of attention without which we would wither and die in body and soul. The less we are touched, the more we become strangers to ourselves and others, and, ultimately, to the world at large. We feel excluded without knowing why. Whoever is no longer touched by anything and anyone dies of loneliness, long before the onset of death itself.

Touch is a source of energy and strength as we grow older. But precisely as our need for touch increases, others' willingness to touch us decreases. Our skin no longer invites being touched, as when we were babies. Old people may appear self-conscious or reticent about being touched, and so others no longer offer to touch them. The truth is: our culture, which promotes and idolizes the fragrant and unblemished complexion, turns old people into 'untouchables', as though touching them would lead to 'contracting' old age and, consequently, death. This is all the more deplorable given that we retain our ability to communicate with the world and others through touch even as our other senses, hearing and vision in particular, deteriorate. And at the end of life, the dying often have no greater need than to hold the hand that holds theirs and dabs the sweat off their forehead.

In order to do justice to the importance of touch in old age, we ought to ensure that everybody be guaranteed a *minimum supply of physical contact* – something that falls within the purview of self care as long as we are capable of it, and within the purview of caregiving when we can no longer do it ourselves. This applies, first and foremost, to *physical* touch: the hand, for instance, that rests in the hand of another slightly longer than usual, the occasional hug that has nothing ambiguous about it, regular massages and physical therapy, the company of pets, or even the sensation of water on the skin when bathing and swimming, the touch of materials, fabrics and things.

Physical touch, however, is far from the only thing that makes for gelassenheit. Any kind of sensuousness that we experience as pleasant will do it, too: seeing a beautiful face, a painting or a landscape, listening to or making music, singing alone or with others, smelling a fragrance, tasting food, being in motion (as when we take a walk or exercise), having gut feelings about things, which often intensify our experience of the world around us. Our senses literally endow our lives with meaning and sense, and every physical, sensual experience has spiritual and mental effects.

Taking the initiative in bringing about touch is not always easy, for it requires leaving one's comfort zone, and we don't always know how others will react to it. *Being touched* is the passive counterpart to the *act of touching*, and it depends on our willingness to let touch happen. It is especially magical when both merge, as when we embrace and are being embraced at the same time and skin presses against skin and two momentarily become one. Touching the other becomes touching oneself, for in touching the other I myself am being touched as well.

Dancing, for instance, is a good way to physically interact with others in a relaxed manner. That is why creating opportunities for dancing is key when working with the elderly. Of course, just as one can be starved for touch, one can also have too much of it, to the point where it becomes oppressive, as when attention turns into obtrusiveness. Finding the right balance requires great delicacy and intuition.

Touch at the level of the soul or spirit is as important as its physical counterpart. Unlike the latter, this kind of touch pertains to feelings and emotions, which can be triggered or generated by the most trivial acts of friendliness and kindness. Wherever there is no indifference, *spiritual touch* is possible. Gelassenheit, understood as the relative absence of restlessness, has nothing to do with being indifferent or devoid of feeling or emotion. Feelings and emotions are life's seasonings; without them everything would be bland. They are the language of the soul, and they speak not only through words but through eyes, faces, gestures and behaviors. Throughout our lives, these verbal and non-verbal modes of expression define the social environment we live in, making us want to be close to some, while driving us away from others.

It is not always good emotions that come out in all this, for emotions, too, are subject to the law of polarity. Negative emotions can be as damaging to the old as to the very young if we can neither escape nor comprehend them. And the ability to feel probably does not end – even in the case of dementia and similar, debilitating conditions – until our very last breath. Those around us ought to be mindful of that.

But there is yet another kind of touch that also contributes to gelassenheit: the touching of minds in thought. When we engage in *conversation*, for instance, we are touched by others' thoughts and can in turn touch them with our thoughts. And not only in converstion, but in *silence* as well: thoughts can be exchanged without a single word being uttered. In silence, in particular, we tend to be touched by thoughts, by dream images, too, for it is not only the real but the unreal as well that touches us.

Reading is one such form of touching and being touched in our mind. For a long time, it had been associated with the sensual experience of holding a book in our hands and turning the pages. But even our new technologies offer a wealth of sensual experience, as when we type, tap, drag, swipe, pinch-and-squeeze or change the font size in an ebook, which turns a trivial problem into an aesthetic pleasure.

Yet what happens if the life of the mind grows ever weaker with the passage of time, until it shuts down completely? We can only assume that the mind lives on in a different register. With age, some of us experience an aura of incalculable reach that is independent of space, time and reality, and that exists unto itself: how else could the thoughts of those long dead remain so alive? Is Seneca dead? The vast possibilities of the mind do not seem to be bounded by finitude, which alone is reason enough for a profound sense of gelassenheit. Relationships based on love and friendship provide the most beautiful opportunities for it: they enable touching and being touched on the spiritual, mental and physical planes in equal measure. Making sure that we have touching, life-affirming relationships is the seventh step to gelassenheit.

7
LOVE AND FRIENDSHIP, BEING PART OF A COMMUNITY

What helps as we get on in years? "Good-natured children," my seventeen-year-old son blurts out without even thinking. He must know, for, having just quit school, he has two cranky parents on his hands. An unhappy moment, certainly; but it does not threaten the love between parent and child in the least.

For this love is not rooted in the fickleness of chance but in meaningful permanence that is a gift to both sides and encourages the child to no longer act like a child but to take life into his or her own hands.

Children are one of the reasons to be gelassen in old age, for they carry on life and support their parents in practical matters. Thanks to our children we can stay in touch with the times, which seem to be outrunning us faster than we are able to keep up with them. Throughout history, parents have introduced their children to life's demands and challenges, but the ever-accelerating pace of technological innovation has turned this dynamic on its head: nowadays, it is the children who introduce the parents to life's new challenges and demands, for when it comes to using new technologies, they are always one step ahead, having been weaned on them. Being able to keep abreast of the latest technological and cultural developments with our children by our side, we are spared the fate of those who find themselves no longer understanding a world that grows increasingly alien, condemning them to a life of isolation and loneliness. But the love between parents and children may be put to the test as well, as the former reach old age: hopefully, we have planned ahead and made sure not to become a burden to our children.

Aside from the love between parents and children, it is the love between grandparents and grandchildren in particular that can add profound meaning and gelassenheit to the lives of both young and old. Even if we might not be able to see and spend time with our grandchildren as often as in previous generations, modern technology makes it possible to stay in touch across great distances. Many grandparents love being there for their grandchildren, doing things with them and explaining the world to them.

The only threat to our relationship with our grandchildren is if we start reproaching them and rejecting the changing world that is their ineluctable habitat. Most often, though, grandchildren tend to find a haven of affection and gelassenheit in their grandparents, which greatly contributes to their development. Grandparents retell the stories they themselves had been told when they were children. Their lives form a bridge between a family's 'small', private history, which they represent, and the 'grand', public history of the past, which they have partially experienced first-hand, thus being able to impart an embodied sense of it to the young. Together, the grandchildren's waxing and the grandparents' waning lives join the circle of life. Both sides can feel that they are part of a larger continuum, which endows life with meaning.

Reliving the growing-up process with one's own children is the most intense and beautiful period in life – at least that's how it appears to me looking back: witnessing them discovering the world leads us in turn to rediscover the world anew. And what if you have no children or grandchildren? Then it still makes sense to seek the company of children, albeit in a way that does not arouse suspicion. For instance, by *volunteering as a reader* to the students at your local school: this way you will be bringing the outside world to the school and teach the children that it takes an interest in them, while at the same time learning about their interests and concerns. Any kind of social engagement, such as mentoring disadvantaged children, will contribute to their resilience. Children can fend for themselves even in difficult circumstances as long as they receive sufficient attention and encouragement, which they repay to those ready to accept the gift a hundredfold. The elderly in turn feel much more part of ongoing life, and for much longer, if they can take part in the growth and development of children. The new movement of integrating preschools within retirement communities also creates such opportunities.

Siblings, too – if we have them – can become part of our support network as we get on in years. Owing to their intimacy, siblings can share all experiences with each other, be they trivial, happy or painful: there is always someone to talk things over with. Through-out our lives, this relationship is available to us, and we can lean on it even when we have nothing else to lean on. But we do have to make sure not to fall into the one trap that will drive an irrevocable wedge between us and our siblings: the trap of grudges and envy in matters of inheritance. Unfortunately, not all siblings succeed at it; some opt rather to use this belated occasion to settle old scores going back to childhood; others prefer bearing grudges to the end of their days, and no one can convince them otherwise. With each broken relationship gelassenheit can turn into loneliness.

What stays with us forever, hopefully, is our love for the person with whom we have gone through life, or parts of it at least. A life shared with another person is all we need to give it meaning: it is the key to staying young for a long time, and the very foundation of gelassenheit in the face of life's challenges. For life is beautiful and replete with meaning to the very last as long as there is at least one person whose existence makes us happy and who in turn is happy about the fact that we exist, if not necessarily each and every day.

Now, more than ever, we depend on affection and kindness in our relationship with our partner, which can only be rooted in a decision that each of us has to make individually: "This is the person with whom I want to stay together!" Ever more often, we require forbearance: as our memory and powers of concentration weaken, for instance, or as we become less mobile and attractive. Particularly when one of us changes – be it on account of inner bitterness, depression, dementia or illness – the question of whether our love will last until death do us part hinges on our decision to make it last. If the ultimate proof of love when we were young was the promise to "follow one another to the end of the world," and to "grow old together," then now is the time to put our money where our mouth was and actually live that promise.

Friendship, too, is of inestimable value as we grow older. What is left when we retire from a job or occupation? For many, it is the friends they have made. We share precious memories with our friends, we can talk to them, unburden our hearts – within limits, of course, lest we turn our friends into emotional landfills. Intimacy and familiarity constitute the beauty of friendship. A friend is someone we want and expect nothing from, someone we simply like being with. It makes us happy that there is someone we like who also likes us, whom we can confide in and who can confide in us, with whom we have certain privileges and vice versa.

The gelassenheit of friendship: rarely do friends live together, which saves them a lot of trouble, or are sexually involved with each other, which saves them even more trouble. This being said, friendship is not all rainbows and butterflies. And problems can best be addressed if we accept them as part of life. And for the most part, a brief time-out from each other will do the trick. In the course of time, moreover, we develop a good sense for the other's likes and dislikes, what is good for him and what is not, what he does well and what is too much for him.

All kinds of relationship contribute to a meaningful life imbued with gelassenheit — that is something we appreciate more clearly with age. And as we become increasingly aware of this, we find ourselves asking: whom have we lost touch with, and why? was there a reason? are we sorry for it? would we like to know how and where this or that person is today? Or maybe it is too late for such questions, and what philosopher Hannah Arendt, at the age of sixty-seven, started seeing happening around her after some of her old acquaintances had begun passing on is already in full swing, namely: the "transformation of a world with familiar faces (no matter, foe or friend) into a kind of desert, populated by strange faces," as she wrote to her friend Mary McCarthy in 1974, calling this process "defoliation" and even "deforestation," whereby it was not she who was withdrawing from the world but, rather, "the world that [was] gradually dissolv[ing]." That, in any case, seems to have been *her* view of the world, which does not necessarily say anything about the world as such. Making this distinction is something we often seem to have trouble with, and not only as we get on in years: perception is prone to posturing as truth, of which it can actually grab but a tiny corner, as the multiple changes in perception we go through in life sufficiently attest to.

Old *enmities*, too, play an important role as we advance in age: we have to decide whether we wish to preserve them to the very last. There might still be time to seek reconciliation, if only in deference to the commandment to "love thine enemy," which is so central to Christian ethics. Living by it, however, requires such superhuman powers that it would seem more sensible not to attempt to bury time-tested hatchets, but rather keep them in play in a civilized manner. For don't enmities give our lives continuity – often more so than other kinds of relationship? Doesn't an enemy deserve our sincere recognition for having been so steadfast a foe over the years? Hasn't experiencing anger and rage allowed us to more deeply appreciate love and joy? Hasn't it been particularly rewarding to have been fortunate enough to be loved by others against the backdrop of an enduring feud? Moreover, we all know that enmities have the power to incite us to do great things, which might have been much harder to accomplish otherwise: "I will prove it to him!" Or is this too petty a thought? Should I myself be in need of a bit more gelassenheit and serenity, both of which expand the soul?

8

GELASSENHEIT AND
SERENITY THROUGH
MINDFULNESS

Mindfulness is the eighth step to gelassenheit. It helps when important questions are
looming. Mindfulness implies searching for
meaning, for context and coherence, and it
allows us to find both: "Now it all makes
sense to me!" The meaning we are dealing
with here is rarely the *meaning of life*, but
rather *meaning in life*, the meaning and signif-

icance of particular phenomena and experiences. What can I myself do to enhance the different layers of meaning? Bodily meaning, which is rooted in sense experience; spiritual meaning, which is rooted in felt relationships; intellectual meaning, which is rooted in thought.

Our thoughts, in particular, tend to encompass life as a whole as we grow older – hopefully, not in order to regret anything about the past, but in order to recollect it and put it in context such that it *makes sense* to us. Having reached the time of plenitude and fulfillment, we can now survey our life in its entirety, interpret, weigh and assess it: where do we come from, what paths have we taken, what have we achieved? what have been our most important relationships and experiences, dreams and ideas, values and habits, fears and hurts, and what have been the most beautiful things in our life?

What used to be a confused jumble of experiences, now acquires definite contours. No one can ever claim to have a comprehensive view of his own life, least of all of life as a whole; we can never be completely certain about its meaning or lack thereof. However, it is not life's objective truth that is in question, but rather the persuasiveness of its subjectively experienced truth. Something inside us demands an interpretation that will support and be supported by our life; hardly anybody will be indifferent to how he has lived his life. And whatever our respective faiths may say, the truth is: *our own interpretation of our life is the supreme court of existence; only to ourselves do we have to justify our life.*

Watershed moments again move into ken, when life could have taken a different turn – biography in the conditional tense: "What might have been if …" Was it pure chance that things turned out the way they did? Was it our doing? Did someone guide us? What do we owe to others? And if so, to whom? What opportunities have we been able to realize in life and work? Did we fight for what we believed was right? Has it been a good life, and would we live it again? Has it been a fulfilled life? What was beautiful and what was not? Which dreams became reality and which did not? Where did we succeed or fail?

Sometimes, things went wrong without our doing; at other times, we could have made better decisions. Pondering these issues for a little while makes sense, but not for too long, for there were reasons why we made the choices we made, and we did not have the knowledge and experience we have today then. And even if not everything was a success, there is no reason to regret it: it is not as though life must have been successful in every detail. It is never a big deal if something fails; what is bad – or at least a real shame – is not to have tried. Failure, too, can be valuable – if not for ourselves, then perhaps for others, who will now have a better sense as to what works and what doesn't, a point of reference for the present and future.

But we do not only *look back*, we also *look ahead* in a new way, beyond the confines of our own existence. What will remain of all that was so important? Does it really matter whether anything will remain at all? What can we do about it? Not in the distant future, but right now is the time to revisit and recalibrate past and present, and to make provisions concerning our worldly belongings, which nowadays encompass both material and digital possessions.

Reflection and recollection can help us to release inner tension and attain a state of *serene acceptance*, rather than succumbing to end-of-life stress. Looking for meaning and coherence leads to answers that clear up and explain aspects of our lives that now make sense as parts in a continuous narrative. For the pre-Socratic philosopher Democritus, who was the first to explain the world in terms of the movement of elementary particles he called *atoms*, mindfulness was the cause of a cheerful serenity or *euthymia*. Democritus' cheerful serenity, which he considered the highest inner good, far above any material possession and sensual gratification, became so legendary that he went down in history as the laughing philosopher.

Certainly, having a sense of humor, being able to laugh, is one of the features of serenity. But we cannot laugh incessantly. Serenity is not the same as being upbeat and in good spirits, even though there might be some overlap. Being able to say about yourself, "I am an upbeat person," does not mean that you have to be upbeat all the time. Mood and state of mind tend to be dependent on particular occasions and life phases, whereas the happiness of the cheerful person is a *happiness of plenitude*, which contains much more than simply life in any given moment. It resembles the happiness of the child, and indeed we can regain the child's sense of fulfillment and freedom in old age, albeit coupled with gratitude for all that has been, and enriched by a panoramic view of life rooted in decades' worth of experience: the many years in which this 'I' that we are has grown and matured; the countless places and spaces we have traversed; all the roads, byways and detours that in hindsight reveal themselves as the most suspenseful part of our journey. And it is only thanks to the long road we have traveled – overcoming many an obstacle along the way – that we have been able to attain this rich, autumnal plenitude that encompasses life in its entirety, with all its positive and negative, agreeable and disagreeable, superficial and abyssal facets.

Being in fundamental accord with life, if not necessarily with every single detail in it, is the basic modality of serenity, which is imbued with a wholehearted trust in life, supplying the self with what it needs and providing it with the means to deal with all else. Being in accord with life outweighs all the ills of old age. This accord goes hand in hand with gelassenheit, which is not hard, deriving as it does from the verb 'lassen' ('let' in German), which in turn becomes easier as the going gets tougher: letting things happen rather than making them more complicated than they already are; yielding to others and letting them get on with it; loosening up in unison with life's rhythms; freely bidding farewell to what cannot abide; entrusting ourselves to what is to come, to the point of welcoming the catastrophe that life is bound for in whatever shape or form.

Certainly, not everything needs to be viewed with gelassenheit, but why get angry now? On occasion, perhaps, for the sake of contrast. Even gelassenheit needs to breathe: its exhalation will then be the time-out it occasionally needs to take. Breathing in deeply, however, means that we can now speak our mind more freely and in a more gelassen way than before, for we have nothing to lose anymore. Ours is the *clement freedom* of old age, as opposed to the *aggressive freedom* of youth; after all, our testosterone levels have been steadily falling. Everything is freestyle now, no more short programs. We no longer have to prove ourselves, not to ourselves, not to others – and even if we did, it would be too late.

Now it becomes incrementally possible for the proverbial *wisdom* of old age to accrue

– virtually without our doing – if only because we no longer have the strength to deal with nonsense. For wise is he who knows how to live with whatever is available to him in any given moment. Even unhappy circumstances will carry their reward for him: "I can learn something from it." He has learned a great deal in the course of his life, and knows a great deal; but he also knows that all knowledge is relative. With keen prudence he can gauge the current state of affairs in any given situation, as well as future developments. He has seen the range of human possibility and impossibility, and knows a thing or two about life's recurring patterns. This enables him to view life as if from outside, with the distance of gelassenheit, which he all too often lacked as a hotheaded youth.

Cheerful gelassenheit does not preclude sadness: being in accord with life and aging includes that, too. Every night, before going to bed, I feel deep gratitude for this day that is coming to an end – and, simultaneously, profound sadness about its having gone by.

The threshold of night reminds me ever more frequently of the looming threshold ahead. My whole life contracts into this one day, which is straining toward night, which might simply be the night preceding another day — which is but cold comfort to me. Looking ahead to the conclusion of the great day of life itself, I am asking myself how I can attain the ultimate balance and be ready for crunch time, how I can complete the work of living joyfully, and hold it up against the grief of having to bid it farewell.

9

RELATING TO DEATH,
AND LIVING WITH IT

❧

Gelassenheit is what we stand to gain with age. The ninth step to gelassenheit consists in developing a stance toward life's ultimate limit, which is closing in on us. Ever more often we are confronted with the death of others, which hits close to home – very close at times – and we catch ourselves thinking: "At least it's over for him." And if our parents are no longer with us, it is clear that from now on we are the vanguard, no more buffer zones between the here and the hereafter.

What deeply impressed me about my own mother was her gelassenheit – not only in growing old, but even more so in the face of death, to the very last day, on which she said: "I know where I am going." She had not the slightest doubt that she would see her beloved husband, my father, again, who had passed on years before and who had always proclaimed that "we postpone dying until the very end." Even as he lay dying, my father told my siblings, who were gathered at his bedside: "I will show you now how to die." My father died at the age of eighty-four, my mother at the age of eighty-eight. My grand-parents lived to be much older: is this my target range?

Not only life but death, too, is a matter of interpretation. What it really is, nobody knows. That is probably what makes it so disconcerting. Only how we interpret it can provide some measure of comfort. It can be viewed as an event that gives life meaning in marking the boundary absent which life would have no value. For only that which is of limited supply is precious, which is why gems are more precious than pebbles. Because our time is limited, we strive for a *gem-kind-of-life* that will contain, in condensed fashion, all the beautiful moments we will have gathered in the time allotted to us. If we are not sufficiently aware of the boundedness of life, we might wind up with a *pebble-kind-of-life* consisting of an infinite concatenation of moments in gray. Because we recognize the temporal limits of our existence, we are motivated to make something of our lives — within the realm of the possible. And should extending life's boundaries *ad infinitum* become possible one day, then many of us would probably wind up *waiting for life to happen*: for why take on the difficult task of realizing our potential, or even dragging ourselves out of bed in the morning, if all that can be indefinitely postponed?

But can death itself also die? In 2009, the Nobel Prize for medicine was awarded for the discovery of the work performed by *telomeres* in living cells. Telomeres form a kind of protective cap around the tip of each chromatid, thus protecting our chromosomes from deterioration and securing cell reproduction. With age, these telomeres wear out, until reproduction stops completely. This means that telomeres regulate aging and dying. However, *telomerase*, the 'fountain-of-youth enzyme', is capable of fixing worn-out telomeres: this happens naturally in our stem cells, which can thus be said to be immortal. Telomerase drugs could induce the repair process artificially, and following a sufficient number of animal trials, we might expect to see the first human trials in the not-too-distant future. Hasn't the possibility of rejuvenation been an age-old dream of humanity? So where is the problem? Telomerase treatment might inadvertently cause cancer, to name only one possible side effect, for it would also contribute to the infinite reproduction of cancer cells.

Death, then, might stubbornly persist in its desire to live. One feature of the inscrutable nature of death could be that it would not exist in the first place if it had not proven a sensible and productive element in the evolutionary process. Each individual thing must pass for life as whole to go on. This does not only apply to me but to everyone else, every living organism, even if we humans tend to think of death as the most insensible aspect of life. Death cuts off each individual life to make room for new life, whose genes will be mixed and blended afresh such that it will be able, with renewed vigor, to realize new possibilities and solve old problems in new ways, or again be crushed by them. From the standpoint of evolution, this model is noticeably more successful than the infinite reproduction of paramecia.

As long as there is death, however, each of us must make a final decision, for death, too, has long been modernized: to the extent that it is still possible to simply *let it happen* – as in pre-modern times – I choose this option. Should complications arise that I can no longer deal with, however, then I ask my relatives ahead of time to decide for me. They know me and what I would prefer *in extremis*. Some of us will have provided more specific instructions, without, however, being able to anticipate the various scenarios in every detail.

Active suicide is also a possibility. For a long time it was shunned in Western culture, but penalizing those who chose this option revealed itself as exceedingly difficult over time. This form of suicide can go hand in hand with *passive euthanasia* if we decide to ask for, or indeed require, the help of others, for instance in obtaining the necessary means for it. And while full responsibility for carrying it out rests solely with us, it would behoove us to give special consideration: to *ourselves*, insofar as it might not be fair to inflict such violence upon ourselves and, in particular, insofar as we might be disregarding those voices within us that might think otherwise; and to *others*, insofar as we might not have sufficiently considered what this step might mean for them. Might our suicide put a heavy spiritual and material burden on them? Or might this actually be our real, unspoken goal – saddling them with difficulties and leaving them with endless questions about our reasons for ending our life this way? For death by suicide, above all other kinds, puts the survivor in a state of perpetual disquiet: was it my fault? what did I do wrong? did I overlook something? what could I have done?

Passive suicide is yet another option. It is based on a personal decision, but does not involve any action, as for instance when a person stops eating and drinking. Suicide is also passive when *active euthanasia* is sought out, which has its own problems, as, inevitably, others will be put in the position of having to assume responsibility for life and death. Precautionary considerations concerning

both the one administering and the one re-
ceiving euthanasia necessitate legal regula-
tions in order to preclude any doubts as to
whether, in any given case, the patient's
death was his own choice or had been ac-
tively pursued by others eager to get their
hands on an inheritance, for instance. Regu-
lations such as have long been in place in the
Netherlands seem sensible: a person's wish
to die must be well considered and repeat-
edly affirmed so as to exclude the possibility
of acting in a state of emotional turmoil; an
illness must be diagnosed as terminal by at
least two physicians; and only a physician
may administer euthanasia.

Giving dying some thought ahead of time
is particularly advisable in view of the many
modern ways of bringing it about. But *med-
itating on death* had already been a standard
philosophical exercise since the age of Pytha-
goras in the sixth century B.C.E. The goal
was to consider life from the vantage point
of its final limit and be able to evaluate and,
potentially, change it. I myself often think of

my final day, my final hour, especially when falling asleep at night or when taking a nap. It is certain that this final moment will come; what is uncertain is what it will be like. It is impossible to know where and how exactly *it* will happen, even if I plan for it. But I can at least imagine it. What for? In order to overcome the fear of death? I haven't managed to do so just yet – death still appears as something terrible to me. What for then? In order to familiarize myself with its utter strangeness, and in order to gain clarity, against the foil of death, as to what is truly important to me in life.

I imagine death as the end of time, the end of the world – for me at least. When my final day breaks, I want it to be a regular day – just the way I like it. Only, on this day I will no longer be working. As usual, I will briefly meditate in bed, addressing myself to an invisible interlocutor – my way of being religious. After a long shower, I will enjoy a delicious bowl of cereal while reading the paper. Then I will stroll to one of my favorite cafés, the one that has thirty or forty kinds of coffee to choose from. I will go for a mild variety – Ecuador Vilcabamba from the Valley of Longevity – and I would certainly love to be able to reach the ripe old age implied in the name. With my cup of coffee I will have something I do not normally have: a sweet slice of cherry pie. There will still be a little time left to pay a visit to the closest relatives of the species that I will have belonged to in life. And so I will stroll over to the primates in the zoo and marvel at how much we have in common, and how inconspicuous initial differences gradually evolved into distinctive features – just think of that incessant, specifically human, longing for the unknown, which drives us out into the world, and our perpetual readiness to explore new possibilities in life.

All that I will do by myself. Then it is my family's turn. I will have already telephoned my two oldest sons, my siblings and my closest friends to say good-bye. All right – although I have not said it, I know how awfully painful it is to speak to someone for the very last time and to know that it is the last time – I have been there, more than once. I will then enjoy a last *guys' lunch* with my youngest son, which we have always called "gu-lu": hardy food – the kind I used to eat in my native Bavaria, but much more frugal than the last meal in Jacques Brel's 1964 chanson *Le dernier repas*. I only hope that our impending separation will not spoil our appetites, but – as befits a philosopher's family – we have, on occasion, spoken about death. With my daughter I will read Oscar Wilde one last time – she loves reading together – we are on *Lady Windermere's Fan* right now.

Like Wilde, I only regret the sins I did not commit. Perhaps I have had one too few escapades; but, then, I have had the fortune of being able to do many nice things with the woman of my life, and that is how it should be during my final hours. My last night belongs to the two of us. We will fall asleep together, and hopefully I will not have forgotten to speak my parting words in time, or at least to think them: that it was a beautiful life, or (something that has often been on my lips) "Thank you, Lord, for filling my life with so much beauty!"

Whom I mean by 'Lord'? I don't know. It's just that I have always felt that something much greater than I has given me life and has guided me through it. Is it a cosmic force? Even if it were so, I do not believe for a moment that it knows what it is doing. And here is another thought: what if we are enveloped by a boundless ocean that carries us along, expanding infinitely beyond our life, and what if it could be like that again – what if the moment one space closes a new space opens up?

10
THOUGHTS ON A POSSIBLE
LIFE AFTER DEATH

❧

Now, perhaps, we begin contemplating a metaphysical dimension in life. It does not have to be, as some would have it, "beyond nature" (*meta ta physika*, as one of Aristotle's works was posthumously labeled). It could also be the cosmic nature of the here and now, which infinitely transcends any conceivable finitude. *Gelassenheit is the feeling and the knowledge that we are cradled in the arms of infinity, and what we call this 'infinity' is completely irrelevant.* It is much more important to be able to be at peace with our own finitude when the end draws near, perhaps even trust, in childlike fashion, that we are part of a greater whole, the way a child trusts that it belongs to the world it came from. It is this attitude that is called for now, there is hardly any other choice left.

Death is the conduit to experiencing transcendence, whether in a religious or secular sense. It is unimportant how things really stand; ultimately, it is not about certainty, which none of us can possibly attain anyway; rather, it is about *interpretation*, and we all have our own – be it on the basis of plausibility (i.e., it has to make sense) or aesthetics (it has to be beautiful). Thus, assuming the existence of a transcendent realm can become the truth of a person's life. And that is the tenth step to gelassenheit: opening our life to an infinite dimension beyond finitude, or at the very least imagining this possibility.

This way, at the point of our greatest fragility we will feel sheltered in a world of meaning whose sheer plenitude wards off meaninglessness beyond the confines of the here and now – unless, that is, we wish to consider this very fragility the fundamental truth of life.

The meaning, the overall significance we are dealing with here is presumably of the most comprehensive kind, joining finitude to infinity. Throughout our lives, we *intuit* the possibility of such sheer plenitude of meaning – in moments of ecstasy, intense sensuality, emotional upheaval, imaginative and intellectual passion, deep conversation or reading, complete absorption in a game or activity, or when we happen to be 'in the zone' or a dream. What is typical of these intense states is that we tend to forget ourselves, lose track of time, and feel universally connected. We often call these kinds of experience *divine*, and they tend to be so intense as to linger in our memory for a long time afterward. The sheer energy we experience in these moments suggests that this might be the very essence of life, which by far exceeds the 'I' and its lifespan.

All meaningful experiences involving the senses, the spirit or the mind testify to it. At the end of life it becomes clear that *energy*, in its various forms, is what distinguishes the living from the dead body, which it is about to depart from. And I do not in any way wish 'energy' to be understood as something mysterious and elusive, but rather as something well known and measurable in its various manifestations: caloric energy, electric energy, kinetic energy. For these types of physical energy at least Hermann von Helmholtz's *law of the preservation of energy*, discovered in 1847 and yet to be refuted, applies: one form of energy can be transformed into another form of energy, but it cannot be destroyed. This means: *energy does not perish*. 'Soul' – which all cultures (except our modern one) have held to be immortal – could be another word for 'energy'. Death evidences that this essential ingredient permeating each organism from the beginning and bringing it to life takes flight in the end. But where to? What happens to the departing?

Life's energy must perforce still be there – since not a quantum gets lost – yet not anywhere in particular. Even on a bodily level, it seems as though there couldn't be any real death: all atoms and molecules sooner or later morph into new atomic and molecular structures, none of them turns into nothing. The body ceases to exist in its present form, but all of its components get transformed into new forms. It might be similar with the soul's energy, and because energy does not age, our souls can feel young indefinitely in our aging bodies.

What grows old is our appearance, not our essence, just as in Oscar Wilde's novel *The Picture of Dorian Gray*: while Dorian Gray's portrait ages, the man himself stays young. In real-life terms, the portrait could be read as the body appearing in the mirror. It ages in proportion to its decrease in energy, which we experience as failing strength. But this applies only to the image that is our body, whereas our energy itself, the essence of what we are and which can be called our 'soul', is not subject to aging. It remains young forever – *forever young* at last, but in a completely different way.

Even beyond death? We could imagine our energy flowing back into the ocean of cosmic energy, whence new forms of life can be filled with energy. This way, the departed could come to life again in other people, organisms and things: life's eternal return. Would this, then, equal rebirth? Perhaps, albeit in different form; so far we have not witnessed the rebirth of identical forms, and even in the age of cloning this can hardly be expected to happen any time soon. What we could imagine is that from within the energy field a new form gets reincarnated, energy becoming flesh and body again. Similarly to waking up from a dream, memories of a past life can awaken in a different body, and that is precisely what some of us sometimes observe in ourselves, convinced that we used to be someone else 'in a different life'.

And as soon as a new 'I' is born, we begin to wonder all over. Atoms cannot wonder, only that particular combination of atoms that one day says 'I' is capable of wonder. I imagine that I will be marveling at all the phenomena and complexities of life to the very last breath, until my 'I' passes and, at a different point in time, another combination of atoms and molecules says 'I' again, which will not be the same 'I'. Can there really be another life, a life after death, after we have dissolved in our current incarnation? Could it be possible to reunite with our loved ones (and, unfortunately, with all the rest) in a different energetic state? There is some plausibility to support such a possibility. Still, thinking (contrary to what we moderns tend to believe) that life will not turn into nothing in the end, but will rather transition into something else and much bigger, must remain pure speculation, though it is the only kind of *trans-humanism* with a great future and no need for futuristic technologies. Transcending humanity, moving beyond it goes on happening all the time – as it always has – in death.

And what is all this for? What is the meaning of all being? If energy is taken to be the essence of being, and if the essence of energy in turn is taken to consist in the manifold possibilities stored in it, it follows that the meaning of being might consist in realizing all of its possibilities without pursuing any particular goal, and so on *ad infinitum*. And if this process ever reaches its conclusion, then *da capo*. Accordingly, the meaning of human existence might consist in realizing all the possibilities of being human – one or a few each, for our lifespan is not long enough for more. Human existence could also be viewed as a dreamlike invention of nature. An absurd invention even? Maybe, but this only increases the desire to take pleasure in this absurdly exceptional phenomenon, to explore the range of its possibilities and to participate in the fleshing out of its reality.

The meaning of each individual human life, then, might consist in the contribution each of us makes to the full flowering of life's possibilities, be it ever so small and ostensibly insignificant, even to the one making it. I am one of the possibilities that enrich life, this is the meaning of my life, from beginning to end. And this goes for all of us. Each experience of every single one of us is significant from the perspective of the whole: evolution as a whole benefits from all of life's possibilities being attempted in countless individual lives. What has been tested on a small scale can then be adopted on a large scale, similarly to the exploration of tourist destinations by many individual tourists: each explores one or a few destinations, sharing his experiences through word of mouth, to the point where all know which one is worth the trip and which one isn't.

Viewed as the transition into another life, death might even appear beautiful and positive. And, who knows, maybe it is but a transition from waking to sleeping. In life, it is not always easy to entrust oneself to this other state. Only toward the very end, when we are overcome by the 'great weariness of Being', does everything work effortlessly all of a sudden. Now we had better trust that not all life ends in death, but only life lived in our present form, which merely recuperates for another life in the *sleep of being* that is death. And just as sleep can heal, the sleep of being, too, may be able to heal life's injuries before it begins anew. Our old life's unfinished business may now be entrusted to another life, which will allow us to exist in a state of serene gelassenheit already on the hither side of the great divide. Having the option to bank on another, new life as we grow older relieves us of the stress of feeling that we must experience everything within the confines of this *one* life. And what if things turn out differently in the end? Well, then at least this – our only – life will have been beautiful.

ACKNOWLEDGMENTS

The publisher wishes to thank the following individuals and institutions: Heather Ewing, Marcelo Guidoli, Teresa Carlson, Licia Carlson and Noah Stengel-Eskin for their input on the title and editorial suggestions; Armin Kunz of C. G. Boerner, New York and Düsseldorf, dealers in fine arts since 1826, for his expertise; and Faye Cliné of The Royal Picture Gallery Mauritshuis, The Hague, for her kindness and generosity.

ABOUT THE AUTHOR

Bestselling author Wilhelm Schmid is one of the world's foremost practical philosophers. In his many books on topics such as 'happiness', 'love', the 'meaning of life' and 'balanced living' – to name only a few – he has created a *philosophy of the art of living* for our time. He has been awarded the German Prize for Outstanding Services in Conveying Philosophy to the Public (2012) and the Swiss Prize for his Philosophical Contribution to the Art of Living (2013). Translated into many languages, Wilhelm Schmid's books have sold millions of copies worldwide. Since its original publication in 2014, *What We Gain As We Grow Older: On Gelassenheit* has topped the *Der Spiegel* bestseller list for sixteen weeks to date.

ABOUT THE TRANSLATOR

An award-winning author, translator and educator, Michael Eskin is cofounder and publisher of Upper West Side Philosophers, Inc.

AVAILABLE FROM UWSP